Puddings &

Arushi Mahajan

A Sterling Paperback

STERLING PAPERBACKS
An imprint of
Sterling Publishers (P) Ltd.
A-59, Okhla Industrial Area, Phase-II, New Delhi-110020
Ph. : 26387070, 26386209, Fax : 91-11-26383788
E-mail: ghai@nde.vsnl.net.in

Puddings & Desserts
©2003, Sterling Publishers (P) Ltd.
ISBN 81 207 2551 4

All rights are reserved. No part of this publication may be reproduced, stored in a retrieval system or transmitted, in any form or by any means, mechanical, photocopying, recording or otherwise, without prior written permission of the publisher.

Published by Sterling Publishers Pvt. Ltd., New Delhi-110020.
Lasertypeset by Vikas Compographics, New Delhi-110020.
Printed at Sai Early Learners Press (P) Ltd.

About the book

No meal is complete without dessert. The most perfectly executed repast remains incomplete unless complemented by a sweet dish. This book presents a repertoire of exotic authentic recipes ranging from the classic to the modern. The recipes are simple and easy to follow. They are accompanied by delectable illustrations in colour, and useful tips for garnishing that are sure to transform even a novice into an accomplished gourmet chef.

The book will inspire you to turn out luscious desserts guaranteed to tempt the most discerning palate.

*To **Badi Mama** and all other members of the family for their love and encouragement*

Contents

Glossary	6
Souffles, Trifles, Mousses and Ice Creams	10
Puddings	46
Fruit Treats	76

Glossary

Almonds	: Badam	Desiccated coconut	: Dry nariyal powder
Arrowroot	: A thickening ingredient	Double cream	: Full fat cream
Brown sugar	: Shakkar	Flour	: Maida
Cardamom	: Elaichi	Fromage frais	: Soft cheese, similar to yogurt
Castor sugar	: Powdered sugar		
Cinnamon	: Dalchini	Ginger	: Adrak
Condensed milk	: Thickened sweetened milk	Granulated sugar	: White sugar in the form of small granules
Cocoa	: Roasted & ground cocoa seeds powder	Grapes	: Angoor
		Groundnuts	: Moongphali
Cornflour	: Corn starch	Honey	: Shahad
Cottage cheese	: Paneer	Lemon	: Nimbu
Demerara sugar	: Small golden-coloured crystal sugar	Liqueur	: A potent alcoholic sweetened preparation

Madeira	: Wine fortified with brandy	*Saffron*	: Kesar
Mascarpone cheese	: Soft Italian cream cheese	*Sherry*	: Sweetened alcoholic preparation
Mint	: Pudina	*Soda bicarbonate*	: Meetha soda
Nutmeg	: Jaiphal	*Skimmed milk*	: Toned, fat-free milk
Pistachios	: Pista	*Sweet potatoes*	: Shakkarkandi
Poach	: To cook in liquid just below the boiling point	*Walnuts*	: Akhrot
		Whipped cream	: Thin, fresh cream beaten till light and fluffy
Raisins	: Kishmish		
Rind of any fruit	: Grated outer covering	*Yogurt*	: Dahi
		Zest	: Rind or outer layer of a fruit

How to make sugar syrup – Mix sugar and water and bring it to a boil on a medium flame. The quantity and consistency will vary according to the recipe. Once it reaches the required consistency, add a pinch of citric acid or 2 tablespoons of milk to remove the scum from the surface. Strain the syrup and use as required.

How to make custard – Mix 2 tablespoons of sugar in 600 ml milk and bring to the boil. Dissolve 3 tablespoons of custard powder in ¼ cup cold milk to make a paste. Add the paste to the boiling milk, stirring continuously till it thickens to the desired consistency.

Hung curd – Take required quantity of curd in a muslin cloth. Hang to let the water drain (for about 20 minutes).

Butterscotch and Banana Trifle (pg.10) →

SOUFFLES, TRIFLES, MOUSSES AND ICE CREAMS

Butterscotch and Banana Trifle

Serves 6

Ingredients

1 raspberry jam-filled Swiss roll (readymade)
175 ml apple juice
¾ tsp ground cinnamon
2 bananas, cut into rounds
100 gm each of white butter and soft brown sugar
600 ml hot custard
300 ml whipped cream

For the custard

600 ml milk
2 tbsp sugar, or to taste
3 tbsp custard powder dissolved in ¼ cup cold milk to make a paste

For decoration

1 banana, cut into rounds and dipped in juice of ½ lemon
Whole almonds

Method

For the custard sauce

1. Pour 600 ml milk along with 2 tablespoons of sugar into a bowl.
2. Bring to a boil. Then lower the flame.
3. Add in the custard paste and stir continuously till it starts coating the back of the spoon.
4. The prepared custard should be of a medium pouring consistency.

For the trifle

1. Slice the Swiss roll and arrange the slices in a serving dish and pour the apple juice over it.
2. Sprinkle the cinnamon powder and scatter the bananas on top.
3. Cut the butter into small pieces and place in a pan with the sugar. Heat gently till the sugar dissolves, boil on a high flame for 2 minutes.
4. Remove from the fire and whisking continuously, stir this butterscotch into the prepared custard. Pour this mix over the bananas, cover and allow it to cool.
5. Whip the cream until it holds its shape and spread it on top of the custard.
6. Arrange the slices of bananas around the outer edge of the trifle and place the almonds in the centre.
7. Served chilled.

Black Cherry Trifle

Serves 8

Ingredients

1 pound chocolate sponge cake (readymade)
425 gm canned or fresh black cherries (seeded)
150 ml apple juice
45 ml brandy (optional)
600 ml hot custard
175 gm plain chocolate
2 tsp boiling water
1 tsp instant coffee powder
300 ml whipped cream
Grated chocolate for decoration

Method

1. Place the sponge cake in a round serving dish.
2. Drain the canned cherries and scatter on top of the cake.
3. Then pour the apple juice and brandy over it.
4. Break the chocolate into pieces and stir into the hot custard until the chocolate melts. Beat to form a smooth sauce and pour over the cherries. Allow it to cool.
5. Mix together 2 teaspoons of the boiling water with the coffee powder and cool to room temperature. Whip the cream until it holds its shape and stir the coffee into it thoroughly.
6. Spoon into a piping bag fitted with a large star nozzle and pipe out rosettes on top of the custard. Sprinkle the grated chocolate on top.

Citrus Ginger Trifle

Serves 8

Ingredients

1 pound ginger cake (readymade)
320 gm canned orange segments in juice
4 tbsp red wine
Juice and finely grated rind of 2 lemons
75 gm castor sugar
150 ml white wine
600 ml double cream

For decoration

Orange and lemon rind

Method

1. Cut the ginger cake into cubes and arrange in the bottom of a serving dish.
2. Drain the oranges and combine the juice with the wine. Pour over the cubed ginger cake.
3. Then scatter the orange segments over the cake.
4. Mix the lemon juice, white wine, sugar and lemon rind in a bowl and stir to dissolve the sugar.
5. Whip the cream until it is firm, then whisk in the wine and lemon juice mixture.
6. Spoon this mixture on top of the scattered orange segments and swirl the top with the back of a spoon.
7. Decorate with the orange and lemon rind.

Traditional Sherry Trifle

Serves 6

Ingredients

500 gm sponge cake, cut into 6 pieces
6 tbsp raspberry jam
4 tbsp apple juice
600 ml hot custard
4 tbsp sweet sherry
50 gm castor sugar
300 ml double cream

For decoration

Small cookie shaped biscuits
Glacé cherries and chopped almonds

Method

1. Arrange the trifle sponge in a glass serving dish and spread the raspberry jam on it. Pour the apple juice over it.
2. Spoon the hot custard over the sponge pieces, cover and allow it to cool.
3. To make the topping, pour the sherry into a bowl and sprinkle the castor sugar. Stir together till the sugar dissolves.
4. Whip the cream in a separate bowl till it becomes firm.
5. Then gradually add the sherry mixture, beating until well combined.
6. Spoon it on top of the custard and decorate with the biscuits, halved Glacé cherries and chopped almonds.

Note: Make the custard as mentioned before on page 8.

Traditional Sherry Trifle (pg.17) →

Rich Chocolate Cream

Serves 4

Ingredients

240 gm bar of chocolate (grated)
1 cup thick cream
A pinch of salt
½ tsp drinking chocolate powder
A little whipped cream for decoration

Method

1. In a saucepan, pour the cream and add the grated chocolate and salt.
2. Heat the mixture, stirring continuously till the chocolate melts.
3. Whisk till smooth.
4. Pour into a bowl and chill till it sets.
5. Serve decorated with the whipped cream and dusted with the chocolate powder.

Banana Honey Mousse

Serves 4

Ingredients

6 ripe bananas
1 tbsp honey
½ cup thick cream
2 tbsp any liqueur (Bols Banana, Baileys)
2 tbsp flaked almonds

Method

1. Peel and mash the bananas. Blend the bananas with the honey and liqueur.
2. Add the cream and blend again. Pour into individual glasses and chill.
3. Serve topped with the flaked almonds.

Ice Cream Gateau

Serves 6

Ingredients

500 ml chocolate ice cream
500 ml vanilla ice cream

For decoration

1 cup thick cream
Cocoa powder
½ cup chocolate flakes

Method

1. Line the base of a mould with oiled grease-proof paper. Spoon half the chocolate ice cream into the mould, press smooth and freeze till firm.
2. Follow this with a layer of vanilla ice cream and freeze again till firm.
3. Keep alternating and freezing the layers of the two ice creams till all is consumed.
4. Beat the cream till stiff. Turn the gateau very carefully onto a serving dish and decorate with the whipped cream and flakes of chocolate. Dust with the cocoa and serve.

Cassata

Serves 6

Ingredients

200 ml chocolate ice cream
200 ml strawberry ice cream

For the cream filling

½ cup whipped cream
1 tbsp icing sugar
8 glacé cherries (quartered)
2-3 tsp vanilla essence
1 tbsp chopped candied peel (orange)
1 tbsp raisins
1 tbsp blanched almonds (sliced)
1 tbsp finely sliced pistachios

Method

1. Chill a mould or pudding bowl.
2. Use the chocolate ice cream to line the bottom and sides of the mould, packing it firmly and evenly with a metal spoon. Return the mould to the freezer and freeze till firm.
3. Then line with a layer of strawberry ice cream and freeze again till firm.
4. Whisk the cream till thick. Add all the remaining ingredients to it. Spoon into the hollow centre of the mould.
5. Cover with a cling film and freeze till firm.
6. To serve, hold the mould over a pan of hot water for a few seconds and turn onto a serving dish. Cut into wedges to show the layers of ice cream.

Apple Mousse

Serves 4

Ingredients

3 apples (peeled, cored and diced)
2 tbsp honey
½ tsp cinnamon powder
½ cup cream
A few mint leaves and cream for decoration

Method

1. Cook the apples in a little water on a low flame till tender, or for 15 minutes. When cool, blend with the honey and cinnamon powder till smooth.
2. Add the cream and blend for a few seconds again. Spoon the mixture into individual glasses.
3. Serve topped with a swirl of cream and mint leaves.

Low Calorie Trifle

Serves 6

Ingredients

175 gm fatless sponge cake (readymade)
175 ml grape juice
175 gm black grapes, halved and seeded
30 mg custard powder
400 ml skimmed milk
15 mg castor sugar
225 gm hung curd

For decoration

Small grapes
Kiwi fruit slices

Method

1. Cut the sponge cake into cubes and arrange them in a dish.
2. Pour the grape juice over this and then scatter the grapes on top. Keep aside.
3. Form a paste with the custard powder and a little cold milk. Warm the remaining milk with the sugar, stirring until the sugar dissolves.. Then add the custard paste and stir till the milk thickens. Cover and allow it to cool.
4. Whip the hung curd lightly and stir into the cold custard. Spoon it on top of the grapes and decorate with small grapes and kiwi fruit before serving.

Charlotte Malakoff

Serves 6

Ingredients

4 slices of sponge cake (readymade)
150 gm white butter
¼ cup sugar
4 tbsp castor sugar
1¼ tsp vanilla essence
3½ cups thick cream (whipped)
1¼ cups groundnuts (roasted and peeled)

Method

1. Cut the sponge cake into 12 fingers. Grease a mould and line it with greased paper. Slit the sponge fingers and stand them around the edge of the mould.
2. Beat the butter and sugar in a bowl. Add the groundnuts and 3 cups of cream. Then add the essence and castor sugar and continue beating till the mixture becomes fluffy and holds its shape.
3. Pour into the mould and chill till firm.
4. Dip the mould in hot water for a few seconds to loosen and then turn out onto a serving dish. Decorate with the remaining cream and serve.

Cottage Cheese Trifle

Serves 8

Ingredients

500 gm cottage cheese (grated)
12 thin slices of sponge cake
¼ cup thick cream
½ cup castor sugar
¼ cup brandy
200 gm bar of white chocolate (grated)
½ cup glacé cherries

For the icing

200 gm butter
6 tbsp drinking chocolate

Method

1. Blend the cottage cheese and sugar together till smooth. Add the brandy, cream, grated chocolate and blend again.
2. Take a flat dish and place 3-4 slices of cake in it. Then spread a layer of the cottage cheese mixture. Continue alternating the layers till all the cake and cheese mixture is consumed, ending with a layer of cake. Cover with a foil and chill in the refrigerator for 24 hours.
3. Stir in the drinking chocolate in a cup of hot water.
4. Beat the butter (it should be chilled) and then slowly add the hot chocolate water, beating all the time. Cover and chill so that it becomes firm.
5. Remove the cake from the refrigerator and spread the icing on top and even on the sides. Serve chilled, decorated with the glacé cherries.

Mixed Fruit Ice Cream

Serves 8

Ingredients

2½ - 3 cups canned cocktail fruits (drained)
2 cups thick cream
1 cup castor sugar
1½ - 2 cups mixed fruit juice

Method

1. Blend the fruits, juice and sugar in a blender.
2. Beat the cream and fold in. Pour into ice trays and freeze.
3. When partially frozen, remove, place in a bowl and beat.
4. Return to the trays and chill, covered with a foil for 8-10 hours, and serve.

Mango Ice Cream

Serves 5

Ingredients

2 large very ripe mangoes
½ l milk
½ cup sugar
1 cup cream

Method

1. Thicken the milk slightly by boiling it over a low flame. Then add the sugar. Keep aside to cool. Extract the pulp of the mangoes.

2. Blend the milk, mango pulp and cream together, pour into a bowl and freeze. After 4 hours, remove from the freezer, blend again and refrigerate. Scoop into individual glasses and serve.

Individual Raspberry and Pistachio Trifle

Serves 6

Ingredients

1 packet mini raspberry-filled Swiss rolls (readymade)
1 packet of raspberry-flavoured jelly
300 gm can of raspberries in juice
600 ml custard
300 ml whipped cream
50 gm pistachios, chopped
Mint sprigs for decoration

Method

1. Slice the Swiss roll into 1" slices and place in 6 individual glass dishes.
2. Make the jelly with 300 ml boiling water and then double the quantity (600 ml), using the juice from the canned raspberries and, if needed, cold water.
3. Scatter the raspberries over the Swiss roll slices and pour a little jelly over each. Allow to set in a refrigerator.
4. When the jelly has set, spoon the cold custard on it.
5. Whip the cream till thick, layer it on top of the custard. Sprinkle the chopped pistachios and decorate with the mint sprigs before serving.

Note: Make the custard as mentioned before on pg.8.

Individual Raspberry and Pistachio Trifle (pg.37) →

Citrus Parfait

Serves 8

Ingredients

325 gm yogurt (any flavour)
250 ml double cream, whipped
250 ml hung curd
100 gm icing sugar
Grated rind and juice of a lemon and orange
1 tsp yellow paste (food colouring)
100 gm candied lemon peel
100 gm flaked almonds, toasted
25 gm raisins, chopped
1 tsp orange paste (food colouring)
50 gm flaked almonds

←

Method

1. Line base and sides of a 1.25 litre pudding dish with double layers of cling film. In a clean bowl, mix together the yogurt, cream, hung curd and icing sugar. Pour half of the mixture into a second bowl.
2. Stir in the lemon rind and juice, yellow paste food colouring, candied lemon peel, flaked almonds and raisins into the first bowl. Stir in the orange rind and juice and orange paste food colouring into the second bowl.
3. Spoon the mixtures alternately into the pudding dish. Cover. It can be frozen for upto 3 months.
4. Whenever it is to be served remove from the freezer, defrost in the refrigerator for 1-2 hours. Serve decorated with a selection of glacé fruits and toasted flaked almonds.

Note: *Plunge the dish into warm water upto its rim for 10 seconds before turning out onto a serving dish.*

Orange Mousse

Serves 4

Ingredients

2 cups thick orange juice
1 cup thick cream (whipped)
3 tsp gelatine
3 tbsp sugar
1 cup water
1 tbsp orange liqueur
A few orange segments

Method

1. Soak the gelatine in ½ cup water and keep aside.
2. Pour the remaining water into a saucepan, add the sugar and stir over a medium flame till it dissolves. Then stir in the gelatine. Allow the mixture to cool.
3. Add the orange juice and chill till the mixture becomes thick and syrupy.
4. Then add the liqueur and fold in the whipped cream.
5. Pour into a glass bowl and chill.
6. Serve decorated with the orange segments.

Peach Ice Cream

Serves 2

Ingredients

4 ripe peaches
½ cup each of condensed milk and whipped cream
½ tsp lemon juice, A little cold water
Sugar to taste
Few slices of peach for decoration

Method

1. Dip the peaches for 1-2 minutes in boiling water. Then peel and mash well. Blend with the condensed milk, 2 tablespoons cold water, lemon juice and sugar till smooth.

2. Then add the cream and blend for 10 more seconds. Freeze till firm.

3. Scoop into individual glasses, top with the slices of peach and serve.

PUDDINGS

Lemon Melon Pudding

Serves 6

Ingredients

---

4 tbsp lemon juice
500 gm ripe melon (peeled, seeded and cubed)
2 tsp gelatine
2 tbsp honey
¼ tsp lemon essence
Yellow food colouring
4 slices of pineapple
Water

Method

1. Sprinkle the gelatine in about half a cup of water and keep aside for 10 minutes.
2. Pour a cup of water into a pan, add the honey to it and place on the fire. Add the gelatine mixture to it and stir till the gelatine dissolves. Remove from the fire.
3. Add the lemon essence, lemon juice and yellow colouring to the mixture and keep aside till it is almost set.
4. Chop the pineapple. Mix the ripe cubed melon and chopped pineapple and put in a glass bowl. Pour in the gelatine mixture and chill till it sets.

Sweet Sponge Summer Pudding

Serves 4

Ingredients

175 gm strawberries
560 gm raspberries
225 gm slab Madeira cake or sponge cake
142 ml strawberry flavoured yogurt
Few strips of lime peel (optional)
Water

Method

1. Place the strawberries and 450 gm of raspberries in a pan with 300 ml water. Heat gently, bring slowly to the boil, remove from the fire. Try not to break up the fruit. Allow to cool.
2. Cut the cake into ¼" slices, then into strips. Arrange around the sides and base of 4 teacups. Trim the excess.
3. Strain the juice from the fruit. Dip each piece of cake into the juice, then rearrange in the cups.
4. Pile the fruit into the cups, pour over any remaining juice. Cover with cling film and chill overnight.
5. To serve: remove the film, turn the cups upside down on plates, shake the cup and plate together to release the pudding.
6. Top each pudding with a large spoonful of yogurt, some strawberries and a few strips of peel, if desired.

Sweet Potato Supreme

Serves 3

Ingredients

200 gm sweet potatoes (boiled and peeled)
6 tsp honey
½ tsp each of vanilla essence and ground cinnamon
3 tbsp skimmed milk
4 tbsp pineapple juice
4 tsp desiccated coconut

Method

1. Mash the sweet potatoes. Add the milk, honey, essence and cinnamon. Blend the mixture and pour into a bowl. Then pour in the pineapple juice and mix.
2. Sprinkle the coconut over it. Chill and serve.

Chocolate Fudge Pudding

Serves 6

Ingredients

4 tsp cocoa
4 cups milk
6 tbsp sugar
3 tbsp flour
3 tbsp butter or refined oil
1 cup cream, whipped

Method

1. Heat the milk and add the sugar and cocoa. Keep aside.
2. Heat the butter or oil in a pan and add the flour. Fry slightly and remove from the fire.
3. When the butter-flour mixture has cooled, add the milk and place it on the fire again.
4. Allow the milk to boil and keep stirring till the mixture thickens and becomes smooth.
5. Pour into a greased cake dish and steam it for 20 minutes.
6. Chill and serve with the whipped cream.

Chocolate Ginger Cream

Serves 6

Ingredients

2 tbsp drinking chocolate
12 ginger biscuits (powdered)
½ cup castor sugar
A few drops of vanilla essence
½ cup milk
1 cup thick cream (whipped)
4 tsp cornflour
Whipped cream for decoration

Method

1. Make a paste of the cornflour in a little milk. Heat the rest of the milk in a saucepan, adding the drinking chocolate and half the sugar.
2. When the milk begins to boil, add the cornflour paste and cook, stirring till the mixture thickens. Keep aside to cool.
3. Whip the cream, adding the rest of the sugar and essence. Fold this into the chocolate custard.
4. Take a glass dish and spread a layer of powdered biscuits, followed by the custard. Keep on alternating the layers ending with the chocolate custard.
5. Cover with a foil and chill for 6-8 hours. Serve, decorated with the whipped cream.

Apple Betty Pie

Serves 6

Ingredients

For the dough

3 cups flour, 150 gm white butter
6 tbsp castor sugar, A pinch of salt
Ice-cold water

For the filling

1 kg apples, peeled and chopped
¼ tsp cinnamon powder
¼ tsp nutmeg powder
¾ cup sugar, or to taste

½ cup water, 2 tbsp milk
½ cup roasted and coarsely chopped almonds
Juice of ½ lemon

Method

1. Mix all the ingredients for the dough except the water and rub the mixture till it resembles fine breadcrumbs.
2. Then add the water, little by little, to knead it into a soft dough. Cover and refrigerate for 15 minutes.
3. Line the bottom of a detachable tin with this dough, keeping aside a little for making the strips on the top.
4. Prick the base and sides with a fork. Then bake this base for 20 minutes in an oven at 180°C. Keep aside.

5. For the filling, take the apples, sugar, water and lemon juice and cook on a medium flame for about 20 minutes, till the apples are tender and the mixture dries up a little.
6. Then add the cinnamon and nutmeg powder. Cook for a minute and take off the fire.
7. Add the almonds, mix well. Put this filling on the pre-baked base and cover the top with the strips made out of the leftover dough. Glaze the strips with the milk. Then bake the pie for 20-25 minutes at 180°C. Serve hot with vanilla ice cream.

Apple Betty Pie (pg.56) →

Shahi Custard

Serves 4

Ingredients

2 cups milk
½ cup sugar
2 tbsp custard powder (vanilla flavour)
6 slices of bread
½ cup thick cream, whipped
1 tbsp chopped pistachios
1 tbsp cherries
¼ cup water
¼ cup ghee

Method

1. Cut the slices of bread into halves and fry them in the ghee till light brown. Drain on a paper napkin.
2. In another pan boil 1 cup milk, ¼ cup sugar and ¼ cup water, stirring till the sugar dissolves. When the milk comes to a boil, add in the fried bread and allow it to soak up the milk.
3. Make a thin paste of the custard powder and sugar with the rest of the milk and cook it for 3 minutes over a low flame.
4. Pour it over the bread and decorate with the whipped cream, cherries and pistachios.
5. Serve chilled.

Shahi Tukra

Serves 10

Ingredients

10 thick slices of bread, crusts removed
½ cup ghee
1½ cups sugar
½ cup milk
6 tsp rose water
6 tsp blanched and chopped almonds
6 tsp shelled and chopped pistachios
1½ cups thick cream
½ tsp saffron
Water

Method

1. Soak the saffron in 2 teaspoons of milk.
2. Fry the almonds in a little ghee till golden. Keep aside.
3. Pour the rest of the ghee into a shallow pan and fry the slices of bread (cut into halves) till golden brown on both sides. Drain and keep aside.
4. Pour about a cup of water into a pan and add the sugar. Boil for about 4-5 minutes.
5. Remove from the fire and quickly dip each slice of the fried bread into the syrup for a few seconds and remove.
6. Arrange some of the slices in a shallow serving dish and keep the rest aside.

7. Return the pan with the syrup to the fire and lower the flame. Pour in the milk and cream. Stir and allow the mixture to simmer for 2 minutes. Add the saffron, stir and remove from the fire. Add the rose water.
8. Sprinkle some of the nuts on the bread arranged in the dish. Pour a little of the creamy syrup over it.
9. Arrange the rest of the slices of bread on top.
10. Sprinkle the remaining nuts and finally pour the rest of the syrup on the bread.
11. Chill for an hour before serving.

Coconut Mango Fool

Serves 6

Ingredients

½ cup grated coconut
6 medium-sized mangoes
1½ cups hot milk
½ tsp powdered green cardamom seeds
A pinch of saffron powder (soaked in a tsp of milk)
18 almonds (blanched and shredded)
Whipped cream for decoration
A pinch of salt
Sugar to taste

Method

1. Soak the coconut in hot milk for 10-15 minutes. Strain the coconut-milk mixture and discard the pulp.
2. Scoop out the mango pulp. Add the mango pulp to the coconut milk.
3. Then add the sugar and stir till it dissolves.
4. Add the cardamom powder, saffron, almonds and salt.
5. Chill and serve with whipped cream.

Date and Banana Pudding

Serves 4-6

Ingredients

1 cup dates (seeded and sliced)
6 bananas, cut into rounds
1¼ cups thick cream
Icing sugar to taste

Method

1. Whip the cream and fold in the icing sugar.
2. Arrange a layer of the banana slices in a dish. Cover them with a layer of whipped cream. Then spread a layer of sliced dates followed by the cream. Continue alternating till the ingredients are used up, ending with the layer of cream.
3. Serve cold.

Carrot Kheer

Serves 4

Ingredients

125 gm red carrots
½ l milk
100 gm sugar
2 green cardamoms (powdered)
2 tbsp chopped nuts and raisins
50 gm milk powder

Method

1. Wash the carrots. Remove the yellow centres and grate them.
2. Pour the milk into a heavy-bottomed pan. Add the grated carrot and place on the fire. When the milk begins to boil, reduce the flame and simmer till the carrot is cooked.
3. Then add the sugar, milk powder (mixed with a little hot water), and cardamom powder. Stir till smooth.
4. Remove from the fire and add the nuts and raisins. Mix thoroughly. Chill and serve.

Apple Pudding

Serves 4

Ingredients

4 apples (peeled, cored and sliced)
Juice of 1 lemon
A pinch each of salt and baking powder
1 tbsp flour
1½ tbsp castor sugar
2 tbsp butter
¾ cup water

For garnishing

1 cup thick cream
4 tsp castor sugar
A few drops of vanilla essence

Method

1. Cook the apple slices with ¾ cup water, salt and lemon juice till tender. Pour into a greased baking dish.
2. Then gently mix the flour, baking powder, castor sugar and ¾ tablespoon butter into it. Do not stir too much.
3. Dot with the remaining butter and bake in a moderate oven till the crust turns brown.
4. Remove from the oven and transfer to a refrigerator to let it cool.
5. Beat the cream with the castor sugar and essence. Then let it chill.
6. Serve the pudding topped with the sweetened, whipped cream.

Lemon and Biscuit Pudding

Serves 4

Ingredients

Juice of 2 limes
8 arrowroot biscuits (powdered)
1 tbsp castor sugar
2 tbsp butter
2 cups thickened, sweetened milk, chilled
¾ cup thick cream (whipped)
A few grapes

Method

1. Add the sugar to the powdered biscuits. Melt the butter in a pan over a low flame. Remove and add to the powdered biscuit-sugar mixture. Mix well.
2. Take a greased baking dish and spoon the mixture into it, pressing it down firmly. Place the baking dish in the refrigerator for an hour.
3. Blend the thickened, chilled milk, cream and lime juice and keep in the refrigerator for a while.
4. Take out the baking dish and spoon the cream over the layer of biscuits. Decorate with the grapes.
5. Chill again for a few hours before serving.

Bavarian Orange Cream

Serves 8

Ingredients

250 gm orange juice
2 cups whipped cream
2 cups condensed milk
4 level tsp gelatine
2 tbsp lemon juice
4 tsp brandy
A few orange segments

Method

1. Soak the gelatine in some orange juice. After 5 minutes heat gently till the gelatine dissolves.
2. In a bowl pour the condensed milk, orange-gelatine mix, brandy and lemon juice. Whip the mixture very well till thick.
3. Fold in the whipped cream and whisk till blended. Chill overnight.
4. Serve garnished with the orange segments.

FRUIT TREATS

Pan Cooked Apples and Blackberries

Serves 4

Ingredients

4 apples
Juice of 1 lemon
25 gm butter or margarine
50 gm soft brown sugar
1 cinnamon stick, broken in half
150 ml red wine
225 gm blackberries, hulled

Method

1. Peel and core the apples, then slice into thick wedges. Toss the apple wedges in the lemon juice.
2. In a large frying pan, melt the butter or margarine and add in the soft brown sugar.
3. Then add the apple wedges and cinnamon pieces into the frying pan and cook for 2 minutes.
4. Pour in the red wine and bring to the boil. Lower the flame and simmer for a further 10 minutes. Stir occasionally.
5. Add the blackberries to the frying pan and cook for a further 5 minutes, or until the blackberries have just softened. Using a spoon, discard the cinnamon pieces. Place the fruit in a large bowl and serve immediately.

Fruits of the Forest

Serves 4

Ingredients

142 gm strawberry jelly
225 gm strawberries
225 gm raspberries
100 gm blackberries
300 gm soya bean curd
Mint and fresh berries for decoration

→

Method

1. Make the jelly as per the directions on the box. Break up the jelly, place in a bowl.
2. Rinse and hull the strawberries, place with the raspberries, blackberries and 4 tablespoons of water in a pan over a low flame. Slowly bring to the boil, then remove from the fire.
3. Pour the contents of the pan into a sieve balanced over the already set jelly cubes. Stir to dissolve the jelly into liquid.
4. Drain the soya bean curd, place in a liquidiser with the dissolved jelly and fruit from the sieve. Blend until smooth.
5. Pour the mixture back through the sieve to remove all seeds. Divide and pour into 4 sundae or serving glasses. Chill in a refrigerator until set. Decorate with the fresh mint and berries.

Banana Squares

Serves 4

Ingredients

5 large bananas
¾ cup sugar
1¼ cups water
½ cup butter
1 tsp cardamom seeds (ground)
2 tbsp mixed chopped nuts
2 tbsp chopped, seedless raisins for decoration
½ cup whipped cream

Method

1. Skin and mash the bananas. Add the sugar and water and cook with the butter, stirring continuously till the mixture thickens. When it is ready it will be a sticky mass.

2. Mix in the cardamom powder and chopped nuts. Spread on a greased plate with a raised edge.

3. Freeze till set, then cut into squares and serve topped with the whipped cream and raisins.

Fruit and Nut Cake

Serves 6

Ingredients

2 cups mixed fruits (peeled, cut and boiled in sugar syrup)
or
2 cups tinned fruits
2½ tbsp each of walnuts and almonds, chopped
1 cup thick sweetened cream
1½ cups flour
100 gm butter
¼ cup sugar

Method

1. Grease an ovenproof dish. Drain the syrup from the mixed fruits and reserve. Spread the fruits in the dish. Pour a little syrup over the fruits.
2. Sieve the flour and rub in the butter.
3. Add the sugar and 2 full tablespoons of nuts. Mix well.
4. Spread the mixture over the fruits and bake in a moderate oven.
5. When done, sprinkle the remaining nuts. Chill and serve with the cream.

Banana Cream

Serves 2-3

Ingredients

3 ripe bananas
½ cup thick cream
1 tsp gelatine
½ cup castor sugar
Juice of ½ a lime
A little warm water

Method

1. Soak the gelatine in a little water. Then cook on a double boiler till it dissolves. Add the lime juice.
2. Peel and mash the bananas.
3. Add the sugar and mash again.
4. Add all the other ingredients and beat well.
5. Chill and serve.

Lime and Strawberry Swirl

Serves 4

Ingredients

½ pkt each of lime and strawberry jelly
Grated rind and juice of 1 lime
275 gm hung curd
1 tsp grated lemon rind
2 tbsp lemon juice
300 ml whipped cream

For decoration

Strawberries
Twists of lime
Mint sprigs

Method

1. Place the lime jelly and strawberry jelly in separate bowls. Pour 150 ml of boiling water over each jelly and stir until dissolved.
2. Add 150 ml cold water to each, stir, then leave in a cool place until cold.
3. Beat the rind and juice of the lime into half of the hung curd until soft. Beat the remaining hung curd with the lemon rind and juice. Fold the lime curd mixture into the cooled lime jelly and the lemon curd mixture into the strawberry jelly.
4. Whip the cream and fold half into each jelly mixture. Chill until starting to thicken. Then place teaspoonfuls of the mixture into 4 serving dishes, alternating the 2 flavours.
5. Using a skewer, cocktail stick or knife, marble the mixtures together.
6. Decorate the individual swirls with strawberries, twists of lime and sprigs of mint.

Lime and Strawberry Swirl (pg.87) →

Baked Apple Ambrosia

Serves 2-3

Ingredients

2 big apples (peeled, cored and cubed)
75 gm raisins
Juice of 1 small orange
4 slices of bread
½ cup sugar
Oil or butter for frying

Method

1. Stew the apples with the orange juice and sugar. When cooked, add the raisins.
2. Fry the slices of bread till golden brown. Cut them in half and place a baking dish. Pour in the stewed apples and cover with more pieces of the fried bread.
3. Bake in a moderate oven for 25 minutes. This can be served hot or cold.

Stewed Apricots

Serves 6

Ingredients

600 gm fresh apricots
¾ cup sugar
1¼ cups water
1 tsp lemon juice
1 tbsp blanched and shredded almonds

Method

1. Peel the apricots and cut into halves. Remove the seeds.
2. Dissolve the sugar in water and boil for 2 minutes.
3. Add the apricots and poach till tender. Remove the fruit from the syrup with a perforated spoon and arrange in a glass dish.
4. Boil the syrup till thick and then add the lemon juice. Pour over the fruit.
5. Garnish with the shredded almonds and serve cold.

Baked Apple Delight

Serves 3-4

Ingredients

250 gm apples (peeled, cored and sliced)
1 tbsp butter
½ cup sugar
¼ cup walnuts (chopped)
¼ tsp ground cinnamon
¼ cup biscuit crumbs
Whipped cream or custard for topping

Method

1. Cook the apples with half the sugar till soft. Place in a baking dish.
2. Beat the butter till creamy. Add the rest of the sugar and beat again till smooth.
3. Stir in the biscuit crumbs, cinnamon and walnuts. Pour over the cooked apples and bake till they become golden. Serve hot with the custard or cream.

Peach Ambrosia

Serves 8

Ingredients

8 -10 peaches, cooked in sugar syrup
3 tsp gelatine
¼ cup sugar
2 tbsp lemon juice
¼ cup thick cream
4 slices of thick sponge cake
A few fresh mint leaves
A pinch of salt

Method

1. Take the peaches out of the sugar syrup and keep aside one for decoration. Mash the remaining peaches very well. Add the syrup, sugar and salt. Blend well. Place it on the fire.
2. Soak the gelatine in the lemon juice. When it swells up, add to the peach mixture and stir till it melts completely. Remove from the fire and cool.
3. When it is cool, stir in the thick cream. Blend for 2 minutes.
4. Grease a mould. Cut the cake into long thin pieces and stand them up around the sides of the mould. Fill in the centre with the peach-cream mixture. Chill.
5. Unmould on to a serving dish and decorate with the mint leaves and slices of the remaining peach.

Fruit Compote with Honey

Serves 4

Ingredients

---

450 ml fresh orange juice
Grated zest of ½ orange
2 drops almond essence
2 tbsp honey
250 gm packet dried fruits (figs, apricots, dates, etc)
175 gm fromage frais
25 gm toasted oats

→

Method

1. Place the orange juice, zest and almond essence in a pan and bring to a boil.
2. Add 1 tablespoon of the honey and dried fruits. Simmer for about 10 minutes until the fruits are plump and tender. Allow the mixture to cool slightly, then refrigerate.
3. While the fruit mixture is cooling, mix the remaining honey with the fromage frais.
4. Place the cooled fruit compote in four individual dessert glasses. Spoon the honeyed fromage frais over the compote and decorate with the toasted oats.

Banana Toffee

Serves 6

Ingredients

4 ripe bananas
½ cup flour
1 tsp cinnamon powder
½ tsp baking powder
2 tsp oil
1 tbsp powdered sugar
Juice of 1 lemon (large)
2 tsp honey (optional)
½ cup milk (approx.)

Method

1. Peel and cut the bananas into 2 pieces longitudinally, or in rounds and then crosswise to get 4 pieces from each banana.
2. Sprinkle the cinnamon, lemon juice and 1 tablespoon sugar on them.
3. Make a batter with the flour, oil, milk, honey and baking powder. The batter should not be very thin in consistency.
4. Mix well till smooth.
5. Heat the oil. Dip the banana slices in the batter and fry till golden brown.
6. Heat some sugar in a pan till it caramelises, making sure it does not get burnt. Coat the fried bananas with this sugar syrup.
7. Then place the banana pieces on a bowlful of ice till the sugar crystallises. Remove them from the ice bowl and keep aside.
8. Serve warm with vanilla ice cream.

Mango Marvel

Serves 8

Ingredients

12 bread slices (with edges trimmed), soaked in milk
2 mangoes, roughly chopped
3 tbsp castor sugar
300 ml fresh cream
3 mangoes, chopped (for the filling)
½ cup chilled milk
Assorted nuts for garnishing

Method

1. Blend the roughly chopped mangoes, milk and sugar into a paste. Mix in the cream.
2. Then spread 2 tablespoons of this paste in a rectangular dish and layer it with 6 milk-soaked bread slices.
3. On these bread slices arrange ½ the chopped mangoes kept aside for the filling. Then spread another layer of the mango paste, followed by the bread slices and the remaining chopped mangoes. Lastly, spread a thin layer of the mango paste.
4. Sprinkle the assorted nuts and serve chilled.

Coconut Custard

Serves 8

Ingredients

500 ml coconut milk
½ cup castor sugar
¼ tsp nutmeg powder
¼ tsp cinnamon powder
Cornflour paste (2 tsp cornflour mixed with 2 tbsp water)
A few drops of vanilla essence
¼ cup desiccated coconut powder
½ cup fresh cream
½ cup coconut cream

Method

1. Heat the coconut milk and add the sugar. Cook on a medium flame till the sugar dissolves.
2. Add the nutmeg, cinnamon and vanilla essence and bring to the boil.
3. Then add in the coconut cream and cornflour paste.
4. Cook on a low flame till the paste thickly coats the back of the spoon. When cool stir in the fresh cream. Spoon this mix into the glasses. Let it chill thoroughly.
5. Sprinkle the desiccated coconut on it. Serve this with fresh fruits.

Baked Bananas

Serves 6

Ingredients

397 gm canned mango slices
1 papaya
2 bananas
1 lime
8 glacé cherries
3 tbsp demerara sugar
1 tsp ground cinnamon
25 gm butter
4 tbsp dark rum
2 passion fruits

Method

1. Arrange the mango slices in a large, shallow, lightly greased ovenproof dish and pour the juice over it.
2. Peel the papaya, halve, scoop out the seeds and discard, slice the flesh and add to the dish.
3. Peel the bananas and cut each into 3, then add to the dish.
4. Grate the lime rind and sprinkle over it. Squeeze juice of half the lime on it, then slice the remaining lime and mix in with the fruit.
5. Add the cherries, demerara sugar, cinnamon, butter and rum.
6. Halve each passion fruit, scoop out the seeds and discard them. Chop the fruit into small pieces and sprinkle over the fruit mixture.
7. Bake at 375°F, 190°C, gas mark 5 for 20 minutes. Serve with yogurt.

Baked Bananas (pg. 107) →

Vanilla and Strawberry Bonanza

Serves 6-8

Ingredients

1 cup cream
1½ sachets of gelatin
½ tin or 200 gm condensed milk
1 tbsp vanilla essence
2 cups sour cream
2 tsp strawberry jam
75 gm of icing sugar
1 box of fresh strawberries, halved

Method

1. Dissolve the gelatin in ½ a cup of cold water and slowly bring it to the boil. Stir continuously. Remove from the fire and keep aside.
2. Heat the cream in a small saucepan until warm. Add the sugar and stir till it is dissolved. Do not boil. Remove from the fire and keep aside.
3. In a separate bowl mix the gelatine and cream and pour the sour cream and condensed milk into it, stirring all the while.
4. Add the jam and vanilla essence to it. Beat with an electric beater until smooth.
5. Pour this mix into an ungreased 5-6 cup capacity ring mould. Refrigerate for 8 hours before serving, or till well set.
6. Unmould the ring and fill the centre with the strawberries.

Orange Dessert

Serves 6

Ingredients

6 oranges, 1 tbsp raisins
¾ cup granulated sugar
½ cup water
2 liqueur glasses of brandy or rum

Method

1. Peel the rind of an orange and finely shred. Put in a saucepan with the sugar and water and cook to a thick, but not brown, syrup.

2. Peel the other oranges to remove the pith as well as the skin. Cut into thin slices, removing the seeds, and place in a glass dish. Sprinkle the raisins.

3. Pour the syrup over this (with the rind). Sprinkle the brandy or rum. Serve chilled.

Apple á la Mode

Serves 8

Ingredients

1 kg apples, peeled and chopped
½ cup each of water and roasted almonds
½ cup sugar, or to taste
¾ tsp cinnamon powder, Cold milk
8 bread slices, with edges trimmed

Method

1. In a pressure cooker place the apples, add the sugar and water and let the apples stew for about 20 minutes, or till done. Add the cinnamon powder and finally the nuts. Let it cool for 1 hour.

2. Take a bread slice, dip it in the milk, squeeze, put the apple filling in the centre and form a ball. Make 8 balls like this and keep aside.

For the custard sauce

½ l milk
5 tbsp sugar or to taste
6 tsp custard powder
1 tsp vanilla essence
¼ cup fresh cream
Pistachios for decoration

1. To make the custard sauce take ½ litre milk. Bring to the boil and add the sugar. Take 6 teaspoons custard powder, dilute it in 2 tablespoons of milk to form a paste and add this to the milk mixture. Keep stirring till it becomes thick. Take it off the fire, let it cool.
2. Then add 1 teaspoon vanilla essence and ¼ cup fresh cream.
3. In a serving dish, spread a little custard. Arrange the apple balls and pour the rest of the custard on top of it. Decorate it with the chopped pistachios. Serve chilled.

Fried Ice Cream

Serves 8

Ingredients

8-9 firm scoops of vanilla ice cream
½ cup desiccated shredded coconut
½ cup fine breadcrumbs
1 cup thin consistency sugar syrup
Oil for deep frying

For the batter

2 tbsp cornflour
2-3 tbsp flour
A pinch of salt
1 tsp oil
Water to make a thick paste

Method

1. For making the batter mix all the ingredients together, except the water. Then add the water, little by little, to make a thick paste. Keep aside.
2. Mix the desiccated coconut and breadcrumbs in a bowl.
3. Take very firm scoops of vanilla ice cream and dip them, one by one, in the prepared batter.
4. Roll each ice cream ball in the breadcrumb mixture.
5. Arrange these on a steel plate and freeze for half an hour till completely firm.
6. Take out from the freezer and again dip each ice cream ball in the batter, followed by a coating of the breadcrumb mixture.

7. Then freeze again for at least 1 hour.
8. Pour the oil in a wok and heat till it smokes. Add 2 ice cream balls at a time and fry them for a few seconds, or till the outer covering becomes brown.
9. Repeat the process with the remaining ice cream scoops.
10. After frying the ice cream balls, dip them for a fraction of a second in the sugar syrup and immediately take them out. Serve immediately.

Note: Make sure that the ice cream is very firm and hard or it will melt during the cooking process.

Champagne Summer Fruits

Serves 8

Ingredients

225 gm strawberries, halved
225 gm raspberries
1 papaya, peeled, seeded and diced
75 gm green grapes
1 bottle champagne or sparkling white wine
225 gm mascarpone cheese
½ tsp ground cinnamon

→

Method

1. Mix the fruits and divide as per servings.
2. Just before serving, pour the champagne or sparkling wine over the fruit.
3. Mix the mascarpone cheese with the cinnamon and serve spoonfuls with the fruit.